May 10, 1997
Kim & Cody

THE
VICTORIAN KITCHEN
Book of
MILK & HONEY

THE
VICTORIAN KITCHEN
Book of
MILK AND HONEY

JG
PRESS

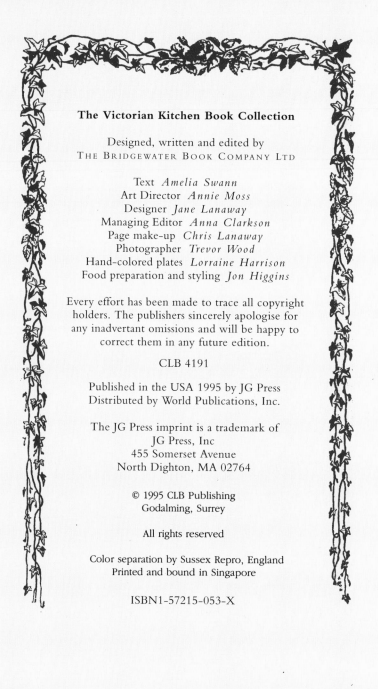

The Victorian Kitchen Book Collection

Designed, written and edited by
THE BRIDGEWATER BOOK COMPANY LTD

Text *Amelia Swann*
Art Director *Annie Moss*
Designer *Jane Lanaway*
Managing Editor *Anna Clarkson*
Page make-up *Chris Lanaway*
Photographer *Trevor Wood*
Hand-colored plates *Lorraine Harrison*
Food preparation and styling *Jon Higgins*

CLB 4191

Published in the USA 1995 by JG Press
Distributed by World Publications, Inc.

The JG Press imprint is a trademark of
JG Press, Inc
455 Somerset Avenue
North Dighton, MA 02764

Color separation by Sussex Repro, England
Printed and bound in Singapore

ISBN 1-57215-053-X

CONTENTS

INTRODUCTION

MILK AND HONEY, the creamy and the sweet, were irresistible to the Victorians, as they are to most of us today. Delicious, delicately flavored creams; pale, shimmering blancmanges; syllabubs; junkets; and rich, brandied custards were all familiar favorites. It was the custom to serve a dish piled with whipped cream, laced with brandy, and studded with candied fruit as an acccompaniment to the main dessert course. For special occasions, Victorian cooks tried their hands at elaborately constructed iced puddings; and ice creams "of which all the fair sex were passionately fond" (according to Mrs. Beeton) came in all

TIPS FOR MAKING ICE CREAM

Here are some basic rules for successful ice cream from Gunter's **Modern Confectionery (1881)**

1 **Too little sugar will make ice cream freeze too hard.**

2 **Too much sugar will prevent ice cream from freezing properly.**

3 **If you want to mold ice cream, freeze it first in an ordinary container until it becomes a thick batter, then pour into your mold.**

ICE CREAM

Ice cream, an invention of the Chinese, found its way to Italy. The 14-year-old Catherine de Medici, bride of French king Henri II, is credited with the introduction of iced puddings to the French court. It was not until the 17th century that the Sicilian Francisco Procopio introduced ice cream to Paris. Italians have always been associated with ice cream; in Victorian England, the ice cream cart, manned by a stalwart, moustachioed Italian, was a common sight.

When she was a little girl, Mrs. Beeton lived in Milk Street in the City of London, just around the corner from Honey Lane Market.

MILK is one of the most complete of all articles of food. From no other substance, solid or fluid, can so great a number of distinct kinds of aliment be prepared, some forming foods, others drink, some of them delicious, and deserving the name of luxuries, all of them wholesome, and some medicinal.

MRS. BEETON

kinds of flavors.

Honey, which goes so well with thick cream, was the main sweetener until the 18th century, when sugar from the colonies of the West Indies became readily available. Even so, in rural areas bees were kept for their wax as well as their honey yield. Honey-based recipes were still used during Victorian times for old-fashioned, dishes such as honey pudding. Of course, you can use honey as a sugar substitute in almost any recipe as long as you remember to adjust the liquid content.

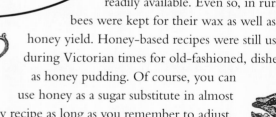

Custard

CUSTARD, TO THE VICTORIANS, MEANT A THICK, SWEET MIXTURE OF EGG YOLKS, SUGAR, AND MILK OR CREAM, COOKED SLOWLY AND GENTLY UNTIL IT WAS SOFTLY SET. THE WORD CUSTARD COMES FROM *CROUS-TADE* OR *CRUSTADE*, THE NAME FOR THE PASTRY CASE IN WHICH THE MIXTURE WAS ORIGINALLY COOKED.

A *land of promise flowing with the milk And honey of delicious memories.*

ALFRED, LORD TENNYSON

A WELL-STOCKED LARDER OVERFLOWING
WITH MILK AND HONEY

CUSTARD FOR ICES

This simple custard is the basis for many ice creams and can be transformed by the addition of any kind of fruit, fresh or preserved, or the flavoring of your choice. Add a few drops of vanilla essence to make a good, wholesome ice cream for children. The recipe is based on one from Mrs. Beeton.

INGREDIENTS

2½ cups Fresh Milk

4 Egg Yolks, Beaten

½ cup Sugar

⅔ cup Fresh Heavy Cream

METHOD

❧ Warm the milk over a gentle heat until almost at boiling point. Pour it over the egg yolks and whisk until well mixed together. Return the mixture to a clean pan and place it on a low heat to thicken, stirring all the time. It is important that you do not allow the custard to boil at this point, as it may curdle.

❧ Once the liquid has thickened sufficiently to coat the back of a wooden spoon, remove it from the heat and stir in the sugar, ensuring it dissolves completely.

❧ Pass the custard through a strainer and, when completely cool, stir in the cream.

Burned Ice Cream

For this paradoxical-sounding delight, add half a wine glass of burned or caramelized sugar to 2½ cups of Custard for Ices before freezing it; a delicious recipe from Gunter's *Modern Confectionery*.

According to the Greek herbalist Dioscorides,
ginger "has a warm, concocting power,
mollifying of the belly gently, and good
for the stomach."

GINGER ICE CREAM

*This rich, spicy ice cream is very good at Christmas,
as a soothing alternative to a traditional English
pudding. The recipe is adapted from Mrs. Beeton.*

INGREDIENTS

1 to 2 T. Ginger Syrup
3 ¾ cups Custard for Ices (see page 8)
½ cup Chopped Preserved Ginger

METHOD

❦ Stir the ginger syrup into the cooling custard mixture.
Place the custard in the freezer and leave until it has
frozen around the edges of the container. At this point stir
the mixture well, including the custard that has already
frozen, until it is well mixed.

❦ Stir in the chopped ginger and return the custard to
the freezer. Allow to freeze for another hour, then give the
ice cream one final stir to ensure the chopped ginger has
not sunk to the bottom.

❦ Keep the ice cream in the freezer until required.

GINGER ICE CREAM, AN UNUSUAL
TREAT FOR CHRISTMAS

BLACKCURRANT CREAM ICE

This recipe is based on one from The Encyclopaedia of Practical Cookery, *published in the 1890s. The author suggests that* "it is reckoned to be one of the finest flavoured and handsomest sweets that can be prepared." *"Cream Ice" was often used as an alternative name for ice cream.*

INGREDIENTS

4 cups Fresh Blackcurrants
$1/2$ cup Sugar
Juice of 1 Lemon
$1^1/4$ cups Fresh Heavy Cream

METHOD

❧ Thoroughly wash the blackcurrants and pick them over to remove any stalks still remaining. Place the cleaned fruit in a saucepan with a little cold water and simmer gently until the fruit has softened. Rub the fruit through a sieve into a clean bowl and stir in the lemon juice and sugar.

❧ Whip the cream until it is stiff, add it to the fruit mixture, and whisk them together for a few minutes.

❧ Place the mixture in the freezer for 30 minutes, then remove and whisk again to prevent ice crystals from forming. Allow the mixture to continue freezing for approximately 2 hours before serving.

COOK'S TIP

For a formal dinner party, decorate this ice cream with crystallized cherries or candied angelica and serve with preserved fruits.

FRESH FRUIT ICE CREAM

Mrs. Beeton points out that a simple ice cream can be made from fresh fruit juice or purée, using equal measures of fruit or juice and cream, and a little sugar to sweeten the fruit. Whip the cream, add it to the fruit, and whisk. Freeze the mixture for 30 minutes, whisk again, and re-freeze.

REDCURRANT ICE CREAM

This is a subtle and unusual flavor for ice cream. The recipe is based on Red Currant Ice, a recipe for water ice from Eliza Acton, which she suggested could be transformed into Cream Ice by the addition of cream and a little lemon juice.

INGREDIENTS

$1^1/4$ cups Cold Water
$1^2/3$ cups Sugar
8 cups Fresh Redcurrants
2 cups Fresh Raspberries
Juice of 1 Lemon (Optional)
$3^3/4$ cups Fresh Heavy Cream

METHOD

❧ Put the water and sugar together in a saucepan and boil together for five minutes. Put to one side and allow to cool completely.

❧ Thoroughly wash the redcurrants and raspberries and pick them over to remove any stalks that may remain. Place the fruits in a bowl and mash them with a wooden spoon. Stir in some of the sugar syrup and test a small amount on a teaspoon for sweetness. Add more syrup, if desired, and the lemon juice.

❧ Lightly whip the cream and stir it into the sweetened fruit purée, then place it in the freezer. Remove the ice cream from the freezer as it begins to freeze around the edges, and whisk well; return to the freezer and allow it a few hours to freeze completely.

BLACKCURRANT CREAM ICE AND REDCURRANT
ICE CREAM, LUSCIOUS FRUITY SUMMER PUDDINGS

*And you're giving a treat (penny ice
and cold meat)
To a party of friends and relations –
They're a ravenous horde – and they
All came on board at Sloane
Square and South Kensington stations.*

W.S. GILBERT

SWEET CHESTNUTS TO FLAVOR
CHESTNUT ICE CREAM

Chestnut
Ice Cream

This *recipe is based on one from Gunter's Modern
Confectionery. Gunter's ice cream parlor in London's West End
was a mecca for Victorian ice cream aficionados.*

She: *I think I should
like ice-creams better if
they were not so cold.*

He: *Should you,
my dear? Then I'd
recommend you to have
the chill taken off
in future.*

INGREDIENTS

$2^{1}/_{4}$ *cups Fresh Chestnuts*
$2^{1}/_{2}$ *cups Fresh Heavy Cream*
8 Egg Yolks
$1^{1}/_{2}$ *cups Sugar*

METHOD

❦ Remove the outer skin from the chestnuts and place them on a
baking sheet in a moderate oven, 350°F, until they become soft.
Remove any bits of stringy rind or skin remaining, place them in a
bowl, and crush them a few at a time, adding some of the cream with
each addition of chestnuts, until a smooth paste is formed.

❦ Add the egg yolks a little at a time and beat until they are well
incorporated. Stir in the sugar.

❦ Pour the mixture into a saucepan and heat gently
over a low heat until it coats the back of the spoon. Do
not let the mixture boil or it will curdle.

❦ Remove the pan from the heat and allow the
mixture to cool completely before placing it in the
freezer. When the mixture has begun to freeze around
the edges of the bowl, whisk thoroughly to prevent any
large ice particles forming, and continue freezing.

GUNTER'S COFFEE ICE CREAM

Gunter's recipe asked for 1 cup roasted whole Mocha coffee beans to be infused in 2½ cups warm cream. Then the cream is strained, sweetened with 1 cup sugar, and frozen.

COFFEE ICE CREAM

This is an elegant, grown-up treat. The recipe is based on one from Mrs. Beeton. It's delicious with thin almond cookies.

INGREDIENTS

½ cup Freshly Ground Coffee
Boiling Water
½ cup Sugar
5 T. Heavy Cream
2½ cups Custard for Ices
(see page 8)

METHOD

❧ Pour a little boiling water over the ground coffee and put to one side to infuse for 15 minutes. When the water has drawn much of the flavor from the coffee, strain off the grounds and dissolve the sugar in the remaining liquid. Allow to cool completely.

❧ Whip the cream and stir into the prepared custard along with the coffee solution, and place in a deep freeze. When the ice cream starts to freeze solid around the edge of the container, remove it from the freezer, break up the mixture, and whisk well. This prevents any large lumps of ice from forming in the ice cream.

❧ Return the ice cream to the freezer for a few hours to complete the freezing process. Remove the ice cream from the freezer several minutes before serving.

COOK'S TIP

Stir the ice cream again during freezing for a smoother finished product.

STRAWBERRY ICE CREAM, THE FRAGRANT FAVORITE

STRAWBERRY ICE CREAM

This fragrant, fruity ice cream is far removed from the bright pink slabs of the commercial kind. It's based on a recipe from Mrs. Beeton.

INGREDIENTS

⅔ cup Fresh Milk
1¼ cups Fresh Heavy Cream
2 Egg Yolks, Beaten
1 cup Sugar
3 cups Ripe Strawberries
Juice of 1 Lemon

METHOD

❧ Pour the milk and cream into a saucepan and bring to the boil. When boiling, pour the liquid over the beaten egg yolks and stir together well. Return the mixture to a clean saucepan and place over a gentle heat until it thickens. Do not allow the mixture to boil, or it will curdle.

❧ Add the sugar, and when it has completely dissolved, strain the mixture through a sieve and allow it to cool.

❧ Chop up the strawberries and crush them to a pulp. Stir the prepared fruit and the lemon juice into the custard and place in the freezer. Give the mixture a good whisking when ice begins forming around the edges of the container, and continue freezing until firm.

COOK'S TIP

This is an excellent recipe for using up over-ripe, though not moldy, fruit, as the softer the fruit is, the finer the purée.

The Wedding Breakfast

For the wedding breakfast they had…six Vanilla cream puddings and Strawberry Ices by the score; but they kept the blinds down in case vulgar little boys should loom in and say "give us a slice," while the leg of pork was being cut.

DAISY ASHFORD,
A SHORT STORY OF LOVE & MARRIAGE

Apricot Jam Ice Cream

This recipe is based on Mrs. Hislop's recipe for Apricot Jam Ice, originally a water ice. Mrs. Hislop was a cook in the household of Lady Shaftesbury. This makes a delicious and unusual ice cream.

INGREDIENTS

3 Egg Yolks
2½ cups Fresh Milk
½ cup Apricot Jam, Sieved
⅔ cup Heavy Cream

METHOD

❧ Beat the egg yolks with a wooden spoon until pale in color. Bring the milk to the boil and pour over the yolks, stirring continuously to ensure they are well mixed. Return the mixture to a clean pan and heat very gently until it thickens sufficiently to coat the back of a spoon. Do not let the mixture boil or it will curdle.

❧ Strain the milk into a clean bowl and mix in the sieved apricot jam; allow to cool completely. Beat the cream until it forms stiff peaks and stir it into the mixture.

❧ Place in the freezer and leave until the it begins to freeze around the edges of the container; at this stage whisk the mixture well to disperse the ice crystals that have formed, and continue freezing.

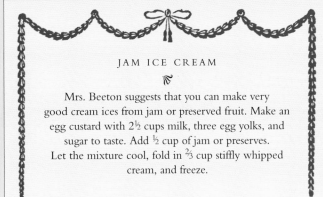

JAM ICE CREAM

Mrs. Beeton suggests that you can make very good cream ices from jam or preserved fruit. Make an egg custard with 2½ cups milk, three egg yolks, and sugar to taste. Add ½ cup of jam or preserves. Let the mixture cool, fold in ⅔ cup stiffly whipped cream, and freeze.

Ratafia Ice Cream

Ratafia cookies are redolent of the 18th century, and so this would have been a "good, old-fashioned" ice cream to the Victorians. The recipe is based on one from Gunter's Modern Confectionery.

INGREDIENTS

1 cup Ratafia Cookies
3¾ cups Custard for Ices
(see page 8)

METHOD

❦ Crush the ratafia cookies in a bowl using the back of a spoon. Stir the cookie crumbs into the cooling custard mixture and place it in the freezer.

❦ When the custard has started to freeze around the edges of the container, stir the mixture well, ensuring that the frozen ice cream is well dispersed through the custard.

❦ Return the container to the freezer and allow it to freeze for a further hour. Give the ice cream one final stir and keep it in the freezer until required.

A half a dozen glasses of Ratafia made him forget all his woes and his losses.

WILLIAM THACKERAY,
ESMOND

Give him three ratafias soaked in a dessert-spoonful of cream.

GEORGE ELIOT,
THE MILL ON
THE FLOSS

VIOLET ICE CREAM AND RATAFIA ICE CREAM, RARE AND REFINED

VIOLET ICE CREAM

❦

This is a very pretty and unusual ice cream, ideal for a birthday surprise. The recipe is based on Gunter's Brown Bread Ice Cream.

INGREDIENTS

2 ½ cups Heavy Cream
Fresh Brown Breadcrumbs
¼ cup Coarse Crystallized Sugar
Crystallized Violets for Decoration

❧

METHOD

❦ Pour the cream into a bowl and whisk until thick. Fold in the fresh brown breadcrumbs (as much as the cream will hold).

❦ Place in the freezer until lightly frozen. Remove from the freezer and beat in the coarse sugar.

❦ Return the ice cream to the freezer until quite firm and decorate generously with crystallized violets before serving.

BROWN BREAD ICE CREAM

❦

Gunter's recipe for Brown Bread Ice Cream is simplicity itself. Briefly plunge a few handfuls of brown bread crumbs into a little hot sugar syrup. Whip up 2½ cups heavy cream, sweeten with ⅔ cup sugar. Freeze the mixture until quite stiff, then mix in the breadcrumbs.

TEA ICE CREAM

Make Tea Ice Cream by leaving out the gelatine from Tea Cream and freezing the mixture. Gunter gives a simpler recipe using freshly made and strained green tea, cream, and sugar, blended together, then frozen.

TEA CREAM

This is a very subtle-tasting, refined sort of cream with a delicate fragrance of tea and a beautiful mottled color. The recipe is based on one from Mrs. Beeton.

> *Love and Scandal are the best sweeteners of tea.*
> HENRY FIELDING,
> LOVE IN SEVERAL MASQUES

INGREDIENTS

$\frac{1}{3}$ *cup Darjeeling Tea*
$\frac{1}{4}$ *cup Sugar*
2 $\frac{1}{2}$ cups Heavy Cream
1 T. Gelatine
1 to 2 T. Boiling Water

METHOD

❦ Put the darjeeling tea and sugar in a saucepan and pour over $1\frac{2}{3}$ cups of the cream. Place on a gentle heat and bring slowly to the boil. When the tea has imparted sufficient flavor to the cream, remove it from the heat and pass it through a sieve to remove the leaves.

❦ Stir in the remaining cream and adjust the sweetness with a little more sugar.

❦ Dissolve the gelatine in the boiling water and stir it into the warm cream. When cooled, pour the cream into a lightly greased mold and chill. Serve with sweet cookies.

COOK'S TIP

Use china tea for an interestingly different taste. Green, or gunpowder, tea is recommended.

ALMOND CREAM

~‹§›~

Almond was a favorite flavor in Victorian cooking. This delicate cream is based on a recipe from Mrs. Beeton.

Perhaps no form of cream is more agreeable or more generally admired than that flavoured with almonds.

A VICTORIAN COOKERY BOOK

INGREDIENTS

½ cup Flaked Almonds

1 ¼ cups Heavy Cream

1 T. Gelatine

⅛ cup Sugar

Few Drops of Almond Essence

~‹§›~

METHOD

❦ Spread the flaked almonds over a baking sheet and place in a moderate oven until they have browned lightly. When ready, remove them from the oven and chop them coarsely.

❦ Whip the cream until stiff and add the gelatine and sugar, dissolved in a little warm water. Lightly mix in the chopped almonds and a few drops of almond essence, and pour into a mold.

❦ Refrigerate for at least one hour before serving to allow the cream to set fully.

ALMOND CREAM AND TEA CREAM, SUBTLE WITH A HINT OF THE EAST

KARL-ROBERT, COUNT
NESSELRODE *(1780–1862) was a
distinguished Russian diplomat and peacemonger.
He helped negotiate the Treaty of Paris, 1856, which
concluded the Crimean War, but is now more
famous for the pudding named
after him.*

King of Cooks

ANTONIN CARÊME (1784–1833), the founder of classic French cookery, was known as the Cook of Kings and the King of Cooks. He began as a pastry cook and became, in turn, chef to the Prince Regent in England, Tsar Alexander in St. Petersburg, and Baron de Rothschild in France. Many of Carême's famous creations for his wealthy patrons were *pièces montées*, complicated edifices of sugar and cake that really were architecture in all but materials.

The Architect in the Kitchen

The fine arts are five in number, to wit: painting, sculpture, poetry, music, architecture – whose main branch is confectionery.

ANTONIN CARÊME

CHARLOTTE RUSSE AND NESSELRODE PUDDING, CLASSIC STARS OF THE ICED DESSERT MENU

NESSELRODE PUDDING

Nesselrode Pudding or Cream is said to have been invented by M. de Mouy, chef to the Comte de Nesselrode. This version is based on Mrs. Beeton, who in turn based hers on a recipe devised by Antonin Carême. She called it "A Fashionable Iced Pudding;" it is certainly a very sophisticated dish.

INGREDIENTS

5 T. Fresh Milk

Few Drops of Vanilla Essence

3 Egg Yolks, Beaten

½ cup Sugar

½ cup Chestnut Purée

1¼ cups Heavy Cream

⅛ cup Chopped Glacé Cherries

METHOD

❦ Bring the milk and a few drops of vanilla essence to the boil, then and pour it over the egg yolks and sugar, stirring continuously. Return the mixture to a clean pan and cook gently over a low heat until it thickens. Do not allow the mixture to boil, or it will curdle.

❦ Remove the thickened sauce from the heat and stir in the chestnut purée. Set to one side to cool completely. Add half the cream to the cold sauce and place in the freezer until nearly set, then remove and break up any large lumps of frozen pudding with a fork.

❦ Beat the remaining cream until it is stiff and add to the pudding along with the glacé cherries. Mix everything together thoroughly and return the pudding to the freezer.

❦ Stir every 20 minutes to ensure no large lumps form, and, when the mixture becomes thick, pack the pudding into a decorative mold and keep in the freezer until required. Turn the pudding out just before serving. Garnish with marrons glacés, if desired.

CHARLOTTE RUSSE

This is a simplified version of Mrs. Beeton's homage to Antonin Carême, the inventor of the Charlotte Russe. In the original recipe, the Charlotte is made in a special mold and turned out when it is set. This version is much easier for non-professional cooks, and tastes just as scrumptious.

> *Charlottes, caky externally, pulpy within.*
>
> OLIVER WENDELL HOLMES
>
> ---
>
> *He would have had jellies and Charlottes Russes instead of mere broth, chicken and batter pudding.*
>
> WILLIAM THACKERAY, THE NEWCOMBES

INGREDIENTS

Sponge Finger Cakes

1 Egg White

1 T. Gelatine

2 cups Heavy Cream

Few Drops of Vanilla Essence

⅛ cup Sugar

Mandarin Orange Segments or Soft Fruit in Season for Decoration

METHOD

❦ Brush some of the sponge finger biscuits with egg white and line the base of a deep, loose-bottomed sponge tin in a circular pattern. Line the side of the mold with more of the cakes brushed with egg white, ensuring that they are closely packed together. When the mold is completely lined, trim the biscuits level and place in the oven at 350°F for 5 minutes to allow the egg white to cook and seal the cakes together.

❦ Dissolve the gelatine in a little warm water and place in a mixing bowl with the remaining ingredients. Beat until stiff and fill the prepared mold. Chill until the filling has set quite firmly, then decorate the top with the mandarin segments.

❦ Return the finished Charlotte Russe to the refrigerator until just before you want to serve it. Carefully loosen any sponge cakes that may be sticking to the sides of the tin, and remove the dessert from the mold.

Swiss Cream

This splendid dessert is an excellent dish to round off a dinner party. It is based on a recipe from Mrs. Beeton.

INGREDIENTS

6 Sponge Fingers or Savoy Cookies
Sherry
¼ cup Cornstarch
1¼ cups Fresh Milk
⅛ cup Sugar
Juice and Grated Rind of 1 Lemon
1¼ cup Fresh Heavy Cream
2 T. Whole Pistachios

METHOD

❧ Lay the sponge fingers at the base of a glass dish and soak them thoroughly with sherry.

❧ Mix the cornstarch to a smooth paste with a little of the milk and bring the remainder of the milk to the boil with the lemon rind and sugar. Once boiling, add the cornstarch paste to the pan and continue to heat for a few minutes until the mixture thickens. Set to one side so that it can cool.

❧ Whip the cream lightly and add it to the cooled milk mixture along with the lemon juice. Pour the finished cream over the soaked sponge and refrigerate until well chilled. Just before serving, chop the pistachios and sprinkle over the surface.

SWISS CREAM

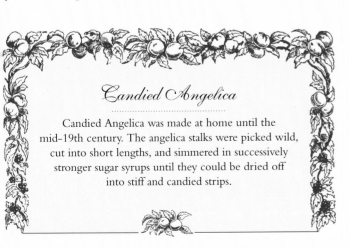

Candied Angelica

Candied Angelica was made at home until the mid-19th century. The angelica stalks were picked wild, cut into short lengths, and simmered in successively stronger sugar syrups until they could be dried off into stiff and candied strips.

COOK'S TIP

If you don't care for pistachios, garnish the cream with strips of candied angelica or citron.

A heap
Of candied apple, quince,
and plum, and gourd;
With jellies soother than
the creamy curd
And lucent syrops tinct with
cinnamon.

JOHN KEATS,
THE EVE OF ST AGNES

Little Miss Muffet
Sat on her tuffet
Eating her curds and whey
Along came a spider
And sat down beside her
And frightened Miss Muffet
away.

NURSERY RHYME

Junket
comes from the
French word *jonquet*,
the little
rush basket in which
traditional country
cream cheese
was made.

GOOSEBERRY FOOL AND DEVONSHIRE JUNKET,
TRADITIONAL, OLD-FASHIONED ENGLISH TREATS

DEVONSHIRE JUNKET

This is based on a Mrs. Beeton recipe, although junket is a very traditional dish. It was once common in all parts of rural England, not just Devonshire, but it was more usually known as "curds and cream." Children thrived on it.

INGREDIENTS

2½ cups Fresh Full Fat Milk

1 to 2 T. Brandy

⅛ cup Sugar

1 t. Rennet

1 or 2 t. Light Cream

½ cup Clotted Cream

Fresh Grated Nutmeg and Sugar for Decoration

METHOD

❦ Put the milk in a saucepan and gently bring it up to blood heat (98.4°F). It is best to use a thermometer to achieve this accurately. Pour the warmed milk into a serving dish and stir in the brandy, sugar, and rennet, and allow to set undisturbed at room temperature.

❦ Add a little light cream to the clotted cream to make it more spreadable: it should be of a consistency that will not tear the surface of the junket.

❦ Spread a layer of the cream over the top of the junket. Decorate the surface with a little grated nutmeg and a good sprinkling of sugar before serving.

Devonshire Cream

Devonshire Cream, or clotted cream, was, according to Mrs. Beeton, "so much esteemed that it is sent to London markets in small square tins." To make your own divine Devonshire Cream, follow Lady Shaftesbury's simple recipe. Mix together 5 cups of milk and 2½ cups of cream in a large bowl and let the mixture stand for 6 hours. Put the bowl in a saucepan of water on a low heat for 4 hours until rings and bubbles appear on the cream's surface. Leave the cream to cool for 12 hours in a cool place before skimming it.

> Chrystal gooseberries are
> piled on heaps
> In vain the parent tree defends
> Her luscious fruits with pointed spears.
>
> WILLIAM SOMERVILLE,
> HOBBINAL
>
> This, although a very old-fashioned and homely dish, is very delicious when well made.
>
> MRS. BEETON

GOOSEBERRY FOOL

Fruit fool is very British dish. Any soft fruit, sweetened, lightly cooked, and puréed, can be mixed with whipped cream to make a good fool, but gooseberries have the subtlest flavor. This is based on Mrs. Beeton's recipe.

INGREDIENTS

1 lb. Fresh Gooseberries

A Little Cold Water

Sugar to Taste

1¼ cups Heavy Cream

METHOD

❦ Wash the gooseberries and remove any tops and tails that remain. Put them in a saucepan with a little cold water to prevent burning, and place over a low heat to cook until they soften to a pulp.

❦ Stir in enough sugar to take out some of the bitterness of the fruit but not too much that it masks their flavor; set to one side and allow to cool completely.

❦ Whisk the cream until it is stiff and combine lightly with the cooled fruit. Pour the finished fool into long-stemmed glasses and served chilled, with cookies.

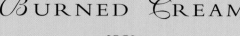
BOILED CUSTARD

This thick, rich custard would be served in individual glasses as a favorite dessert with the gentlemen diners in London's chophouses. The recipe is based on one from Mrs. Beeton.

INGREDIENTS

½ cup Sugar
Rind of 1 Lemon
2½ cups Milk
4 Duck's Eggs or 5 Hen's Eggs
1 to 2 T. Brandy
Fresh Grated Nutmeg for Decoration

METHOD

❦ Place the sugar, lemon rind, and milk in a saucepan and simmer over a very low heat for a few minutes to allow the lemon to impart its flavor. Bring the milk to a boil and strain it into a clean bowl.

❦ Whisk the eggs well and stir them into the cooling milk, and strain the mixture again into another clean bowl. Stand the bowl over a saucepan of boiling water and stir constantly until the custard thickens, but do not allow it to boil or it will curdle.

❦ Once thickened, remove the custard from the heat and stir in the brandy. Pour into glasses and grate over a little nutmeg before serving.

COOK'S TIP

It is desirable to use duck eggs for this custard, if available, as Mrs. Beeton observed, "They add very much to the flavour and richness." You could also subsitute cream for the milk for an extremely rich dish.

BURNED CREAM

This is based on a recipe from Domestic Cookery, by a lady, published in 1848. The lady was Maria Rundell. This delicious dessert is probably better known today by its French name, Crème Brulée.

INGREDIENTS

2½ cups Heavy Cream
Grated Rind of 1 Lemon
Cinnamon Stick
4 Egg Yolks
¼ cup Sugar
Soft Brown Sugar

METHOD

❦ Slowly bring the cream, lemon rind and cinnamon to a boil over a low heat. When boiling, remove the pan from the heat and pass it through a sieve. Beat the egg yolks in a bowl and gradually pour in the hot cream, stirring constantly until the mixture has cooled considerably.

❦ Add the sugar and pour the mixture into a serving dish to finish cooling.

❦ When cold, sprinkle some soft brown sugar over the surface of the dessert and place under a very hot broiler until it has browned nicely.

THE QUEEN'S CUSTARD

Eliza Acton gives a sumptuous recipe for a positively regal custard. Onto the beaten yolks of 12 fresh eggs, pour 3¾ cups of boiled cream sweetened with ½ cup sugar. Add a soupçon of salt, thicken as usual, and, when nearly cold, pour in a glass and a half of fruit liqueur. She suggests curaçao, maraschino, or noyau (almond liqueur), but you could use kirsch, lemon brandy – or whatever you fancy.

*Rich as custard pudding
at a city feast.*

PETER PINDAR (JOHN WOLCOT),
ODE UPON ODE

BOILED CUSTARD AND BURNED CREAM, THE FAVORITE
PUDDINGS OF THE VICTORIAN GENTLEMAN

Whipped Cream

Whipped Cream was served as a side dish with the dessert on all the best-appointed Victorian dinner tables. It was not simply cream with a little sugar; for every 2½ cups of heavy cream, one added ½ cup sugar, a glass of sherry or sweet white wine, a little brandy, if desired, finely grated lemon rind, and the white of an egg. This delicious mixture was piled into an ornamental dish and spangled with candied peel.

SIMPLE YET ELEGANT WHIPPED SYLLABUB

CHOCOLATE CUSTARDS

This recipe is based on one from Eliza Acton. The custards are gorgeously rich, an absolute indulgence for chocolate lovers.

INGREDIENTS

2 squares Good Quality Semi-sweet Chocolate
3 to 4 T. Water
2½ cups Fresh Milk
⅛ cup Sugar
5 Eggs

COOK'S TIP

Acording to Eliza Acton, these custards can be made "infinitely finer" if made with the yolks of the eggs only, in which case the number should be doubled.

METHOD

❦ Break the chocolate into a saucepan, pour over the water, and place on a gentle heat until the chocolate has melted and formed a smooth, dark sauce.
❦ Slowly add the milk to the saucepan, stirring until it is all incorporated, then add the sugar and allow a short time for it to dissolve.
❦ Break the eggs into a bowl and loosely beat them. Slowly pour the hot milk over the eggs, stirring continuously until well combined.
❦ Pass the sauce through a strainer into a clean saucepan and return it to a low heat to thicken without boiling. Allow the finished custard to cool before pouring into small, individual dishes or bowls to serve.

CHOCOLATE CUSTARDS, THE DESSERT TO DIE FOR

In one of Jane Austen's very early works, she describes a catastrophe that befalls her heroine, who has just cooked a huge amount of food for her sister's wedding breakfast. "I never remember suffering any vexation equal to what I experienced last Monday when my sister came running to me... with her face as white as a Whipt Syllabub, and told me that Hervey had been thrown from his Horse, had fractured his Scull and was in the most emminent Danger. 'Good God! (said I) you don't say so? Why what in the name of Heaven will become of all the Victuals!'"

JANE AUSTEN,
LESLEY CASTLE

Whipped Syllabub

This is a very simple dessert that looks more than a little special on serving. Syllabub is originally an 17th-century dish, but this is an adpatation of Mrs. Beeton's recipe, who based hers in turn on Eliza Acton's "Very Superior Whipped Syllabub."

INGREDIENTS

1¼ cups Fresh Heavy Cream
⅔ cup Sweet Sherry
3 to 4 T. Brandy
½ cup Sugar
Juice of Half a Lemon
Fresh Grated Nutmeg
Whipped Cream for Decoration
Toasted Almond Slivers for Decoration

METHOD

❦ Place the cream, sherry, brandy, sugar, and lemon juice in a large mixing bowl, and whisk the mixture until it thickens.
❦ Take six clean, tall glasses and dip their rims first into loosely beaten egg white, then into brown sugar. Allow the sugar a few minutes to dry, then fill each glass with the prepared syllabub.
❦ Decorate with a little whipped cream and a few toasted almond slivers, and chill thoroughly. Serve with thin almond or lemon flavored cookies.

PALE AND LOVELY, VANILLA BLANCMANGE

*Ah, you flavour
everything.
You are the vanille
of society.*

THE REVEREND
SYDNEY SMITH

VANILLA BLANCMANGE

*Creamy, pure and virginally white, vanilla blancmange was considered suitable
for the most delicate or convalescent palates. This recipe is based on one from Mrs. Beeton.*

COOK'S TIP

For a true Victorian
touch, garnish the
blancmange with
maidenhair fern and
a single scarlet
geranium.

INGREDIENTS

2 cups Fresh Milk
1/2 cup Sugar
Few Drops of Vanilla Essence
2 Egg Yolks
2 T. Gelatine
2/3 cup Cold Water
2/3 cup Fresh Heavy Cream

METHOD

❧ Put the milk, sugar, and a few drops of vanilla essence into a
saucepan and slowly bring to a boil. Lightly beat the egg yolks in a
mixing bowl and pour over the boiling milk, beating continuously until
well mixed together.

❧ Return the mixture to a clean pan and simmer over a low heat
until the mixture coats the back of a wooden spoon. Do not let it boil
or the mixture will curdle. When sufficiently thickened, remove the pan
from the heat and add the gelatine dissolved in the cold water, and
allow to cool for a few minutes.

❧ Whip the cream until stiff and stir into the cooling blancmange,
pour into a mold, and refrigerate until firmly set.

This, if carefully made, and with ripe quinces, is one of the most richly-flavoured preparations of fruit that we have ever tasted.
ELIZA ACTON

DELICIOUSLY FRUITY QUINCE BLANCMANGE

QUINCE BLANCMANGE

This beautiful pink blancmange is based on a recipe from Eliza Acton. She made it up on the spur of the moment for a friend, and her surprise and enthusiasm at the finished result shines through her account of it.

INGREDIENTS

2 lb. Fresh Quinces
2 1/2 cups Fresh Water
1 1/2 cups Sugar
2 T. Gelatine
1 1/4 cups Heavy Cream

COOK'S TIP

You can substitute the juice of other fruits to make a different-flavored blancmange.

METHOD

❦ Wash and roughly chop the quinces and place them in a preserving pan with the cold water. Cover and cook them until they reduce to a pulp, then spoon the fruit into a jelly bag and allow the juices to collect in a bowl underneath.

❦ Measure 2 1/2 cups of the quince juice and pour it into a saucepan. Add the sugar and place over a low heat, stirring continuously until the sugar has dissolved.

❦ Remove the saucepan from the heat and add the gelatine which has been dissolved in a little cold water. Set the pan to one side to cool.

❦ Whip the cream until stiff and stir into the cooling blancmange; pour into a dampened mold and place in the refrigerator until set.

RICE PUDDING

This delicious, creamy rice pudding is based on
Eliza Acton's recipe for "A Good French Rice Pudding," or
Gâteau de Riz. She suggested varying it by flavoring the milk or
cream with coconut, vanilla, or ground almonds.

INGREDIENTS

1 cup Carolina Rice
2 1/2 cups Fresh Milk
2 1/2 cups Light Cream
1/3 cup Butter
2/3 cup Sugar
Grated Rind of 1 Lemon
6 Eggs, Separated

COOK'S TIP

It is important
that the oven is at a
moderate temperature,
as this will improve the
look of the finished
rice pudding.

METHOD

❦ Wash the rice several times in fresh, cold water and
place it in a saucepan with the milk and cream. Bring to
a gentle simmer and cook until the rice is just tender.

❦ Add the butter, sugar, and lemon rind and continue
simmering until the rice is fully cooked.

❦ Remove the pan from the heat and allow it to cool a little, then
beat in the egg yolks one at a time until all are incorporated.

❦ Whisk the egg whites until they form peaks and stir them into the
rice mixture. Pour the prepared pudding into a lightly greased dish
suitable for placing in the oven. Bake at 350°F for 1 hour.

A Difficult Choice

MARCEL PROUST, THE FRENCH WRITER, WAS
EXTREMELY FOND OF RICE PUDDING. WHEN HIS
PARENTS OFFERED HIM THE TREAT OF AN OUTING TO
THE THEATER, HE DECLARED HIMSELF TO BE "AS
INCAPABLE OF DECIDING WHICH PLAY I SHOULD PREFER
TO SEE AS IF, AT THE DINNER TABLE, THEY HAD OBLIGED
ME TO CHOOSE BETWEEN RICE A L'IMPERATRICE AND
THE FAMOUS CREAM OF CHOCOLATE."

Yankee Doodle came to town
Riding on a pony
Stuck a feather in his cap
And called it Macaroni.

EDWARD BANGS

SWEET MACARONI

This is an unusual but delicious way to use macaroni.
It makes a satisfying, wholesome dessert and is as economical
as Mrs. Beeton could have desired. The recipe is an adaptation
of her "Sweet Dish of Macaroni."

INGREDIENTS

3 3/4 cups Fresh Milk
Rind of 1 Lemon
1/2 cup Sugar
1 cup Macaroni
2 cups Boiled Custard (see page 26)
Fresh Grated Nutmeg

METHOD

❦ Put the milk, lemon rind, and sugar in a saucepan and bring slowly
to the boil.

❦ Reduce the heat to a simmer and add the macaroni. Allow it cook
gently in the milk until tender but still firm. If all the milk evaporates
before the macaroni is sufficiently cooked, add more.

❦ Spread the hot macaroni over a serving dish and pour over the
boiled custard. A little grated nutmeg can be used to garnish this
simple, but filling, dessert.

Eliza Acton observed that rice pudding could be served covered with a layer of strawberry, apple or any other clear fruit jelly.

SWEET MACARONI AND RICE PUDDING,
NURSERY FARE THAT APPEALS TO EVERYONE

CUSTARD FRITTERS, A DELIGHTFUL DEEP-FRIED SURPRISE

Crema Fritta

CREMA FRITTA, Fried Cream, is a traditional Italian dish eaten at Carnevale, the last day of indulgence before Lent. It is a particular favorite with children.

CUSTARD FRITTERS

These are a light and delicious surprise, very like the Italian dish Crema Fritta. Serve them dredged with sugar and eat them like little cakes or as a dessert, with your favorite sweet sauce.

Good Sooth, she is The queen of curds and cream.

WILLIAM SHAKESPEARE, THE WINTER'S TALE

INGREDIENTS

¼ cup Flour

¼ cup Cornstarch

1¼ cups Fresh Milk

¼ cup Sugar

Pinch of Salt

2 Egg Yolks

Vanilla Essence

Beaten Egg Yolk and Breadcrumbs for Coating Fritters

METHOD

❦ Sift together the flour and cornstarch and mix to a smooth paste using a little of the milk. Bring the remainder of the milk to a boil and pour it slowly over the flour paste while stirring with a spoon.

❦ Return the mixture to a clean saucepan and place it on a gentle heat until it thickens. Stir in the sugar, pinch of salt, and egg yolks, and continue to cook over a low heat. Do not allow the mixture to boil or it may curdle. Stir in a few drops of vanilla essence.

❦ Spread the mixture over a tray to make a layer about ½ inch thick, and allow to cool completely.

❦ When cold, use a plain cookie cutter to cut small rounds from the set mixture. Dip them first in the beaten egg yolk, then evenly coat them in breadcrumbs and fry in a little fat until golden brown. Serve with a sweet sauce of your choice.

CREAM SORBET

This light sorbet is based on a recipe from Mrs. Beeton. Serve it alone as a palate freshener after a rich main course, or with fresh fruit purée.

INGREDIENTS

3 3/4 cups Cold Water
1 1/4 cups Sugar
Juice of 2 Lemons
Few Drops of Vanilla Essence
1 1/4 cups Heavy Cream
3 Egg Whites
Juice of 2 Lemons

METHOD

❦ Bring the water to the boil in a large saucepan and add the sugar. When the sugar has dissolved, allow the water to reduce a little, skimming off any scum that may rise to the surface. Remove the pan from the heat when the water has thickened to a syrup but remains clear; stir in the lemon juice and vanilla essence, and leave to cool completely.

❦ Stiffly beat the heavy cream and egg whites in separate bowls and stir them into the cold syrup; pour the mixture into a bowl and put it in the freezer.

❦ When the sorbet has almost frozen, remove it from the freezer and break it up with a whisk until there are no large lumps of ice remaining. Return it to the freezer and allow to freeze completely.

COOK'S TIP

It is a good idea to remove the sorbet from the freezer ten minutes before serving.

The Digestive Sorbet

During the staggering 12-course royal banquets that were standard during Queen Victoria's reign, it was the custom to serve water ices, or sorbets, halfway through the meal to cool and rest the stomach before the roast meat. In the Queen's kitchens, sorbets were made in bulk and stored in iceboxes. Victoria and the Prince of Wales were particularly partial to rum-flavored sorbets.

ICED QUEEN'S PUDDING

This is a very elegant pudding for special occasions. The recipe is based on one from Mrs. Beeton.

INGREDIENTS

3 3/4 cups Custard for Ices (see page 8)
2 1/2 cups Heavy Cream
1/3 cup Diced Glacé Cherries
1/3 cup Diced Dried Apricots
Toasted Almond Slivers for Decoration

METHOD

❦ Place the prepared custard in the freezer and leave until half-frozen. Stiffly whip the cream and stir into the part-frozen custard along with the diced cherries and apricots.

❦ Transfer the mixture to a decorative mold and return the pudding to the freezer for another 2 hours.

❦ Just before serving, turn the pudding out onto a silver tray and decorate generously with toasted almond slivers.

CREAM SORBET AND ICED QUEEN'S PUDDING, ICES FOR FORMAL OCCASIONS

ICED COFFEE

This is is utterly delicious, a real indulgence for a lazy, languid day. The recipe is based on one from Mrs. Beeton, but she does not include the brandy.

INGREDIENTS

1¼ cups Fresh Milk

1 cup Sugar

Few Drops of Vanilla Essence

⅔ cup Strong Hot Coffee

1¼ cups Fresh Heavy Cream

3 to 4 T. Brandy

METHOD

☙ Place the milk, sugar, and a few drops of vanilla essence in a saucepan and bring almost to the boil.

☙ Remove the pan from the heat and stir in the hot coffee; allow the mixture to cool and pass it through a fine sieve. Lightly whip the cream and stir it into the coffee along with the brandy.

☙ Serve in delicate glasses over lots of crushed ice, accompanied by cookies and a little extra sugar for sprinkling.

Lady Granville's Iced Coffee

LADY MARIE GRANVILLE HAD HER OWN SIMPLE, ELEGANT RECIPE FOR THIS DELICIOUS REFRESHMENT. CREAM, COFFEE, AND MILK WERE MIXED TOGETHER IN EQUAL PARTS, SWEETENED TO TASTE AND THEN ICED.

DU LAIT À MADAME

This comes from Eliza Acton. She reports that it is "much eaten abroad during summer, and is considered very wholesome." Fresh, full fat milk is boiled and cooled, then the cream is skimmed off. The warm milk is poured into an earthenware jug, the cream is spooned gently on top, and the jug covered and left for 24 hours in a warm place. The milk is transformed into a kind of crème fraîche, to be eaten with fine white sugar.

ICED COFFEE, A DIVINE INDULGENCE FOR LANGUID SUMMER AFTERNOONS

CAMBRIDGE MILK PUNCH

This is a genuine university recipe, collected by Eliza Acton. It was served with plain cookies and was doubtless a powerful stimulus to cerebration.

INGREDIENTS

5 cups Fresh Milk

Rind of 1 Lemon

$^1/_2$ cup Sugar

2 Egg Yolks

A Little Cold Milk

$1^1/_4$ cups Rum

$^2/_3$ cup Brandy

METHOD

❧ Pour the milk into a large saucepan, add the lemon rind and sugar, place on the heat, and allow to come to the boil.

❧ Mix the egg yolks with a little cold milk and pass through a strainer. When the milk in the pan is boiling, take the pan from the heat and add the strained egg yolks. Remove the lemon rind and return the pan to a gentle heat. Do not boil, or the mixture will curdle.

❧ Slowly stir in the rum and brandy and allow it to warm through for a minute before serving in warmed glasses.

*For Cambridge people
rarely smile
Being urban, squat, and
packed with guile.*

RUPERT BROOKE,
THE OLD VICARAGE,
GRANTCHESTER

UNDERGRADUATES
*owe their happiness chiefly
to the consciousness that
they are not at school. The
nonsense which was
knocked out of them at
school is all put gently
back at Oxford or
Cambridge.*

MAX BEERBOHM,
GOING BACK TO SCHOOL

CAMBRIDGE MILK PUNCH,
THE ELIXIR OF THE WELL EDUCATED

MILK LEMONADE

Eliza Acton also has an intoxicating recipe for "Delicious Milk Lemonade," not a drink for the children. Dissolve 1 cup sugar in $2^1/_2$ cups boiling water. Add $2^1/_2$ cups of lemon juice, $^2/_3$ cup sherry, and 2 cups cold milk. Stir together and strain through a jelly bag until clear.

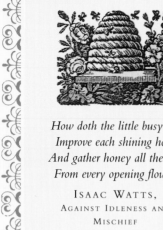

How doth the little busy bee
Improve each shining hour
And gather honey all the day
From every opening flower.

ISAAC WATTS,
AGAINST IDLENESS AND
MISCHIEF

Honey Cake

This is a lovely cake to bake as an impromptu
treat for children – it tastes best eaten straight from the oven.
The recipe is based on one from Mrs. Beeton.

INGREDIENTS

$1/4$ cup Sugar
$1/2$ cup Sour Cream
$1 1/2$ cups Flour
3 to 4 T. Honey
Good Pinch of Bicarbonate of Soda

METHOD

❧ Mix together the sugar and sour cream
in a large mixing bowl. Sift in the flour
and beat thoroughly. Add the honey.
❧ Beat the cake mixture once more,
adding the bicarbonate of soda while
doing so, then pour the finished mixture
into a well-greased cake pan. Bake at
350°F for 45 minutes, until
golden brown.

COOK'S TIP

The amount of honey
given in the recipe is
only an approximate
measure; if you have a
particular liking for it,
there is no reason why
a little more cannot
be added.

HONEY ROUNDELS

These delectable confections tend to disappear as soon as they are
ready, so keep a note of how many you make. They are based on
an American recipe of the Victorian period.

INGREDIENTS

$3 1/2$ cups Sugar
$1 1/4$ cups Heavy Cream
$2/3$ cup Honey
1 Egg White
$1/4$ cup Chopped Marrons Glacés
$1/4$ cup Chopped Candied Pineapple
Few Drops of Rose Extract

METHOD

❧ Put the sugar and cream into a saucepan; boil together until they
reach 240°F. Use a sugar thermometer to measure this exactly. Add the
honey and continue heating until the thermometer reads 250°F. Once
this temperature is reached, remove the pan from the heat.
❧ Beat the egg white until it forms stiff peaks, then add it to the
saucepan and carefully beat together for a minute. Add the chopped
marrons glacés, candied pineapple, and a few drops of rose extract, and
beat together well. As the mixture cools it will become firmer and more
difficult to beat.
❧ When sufficiently firm, take small amounts of the mixture and form
into round shapes. Stand the finished candies on wax paper.

Stands the Church clock at ten to three?
And is there honey still for tea?
RUPERT BROOKE,
THE OLD VICARAGE, GRANTCHESTER

THE GOLDEN DELIGHTS OF
HONEY CAKE AND ANGEL FOOD FUDGE

ANGEL FOOD FUDGE

*This blissful, honey-based fudge comes from an authentic Victorian recipe. Packed in an elegant box,
it would make a wonderful gift for friends who can resist anything but temptation.*

INGREDIENTS

⅔ cup Clear Honey
2¼ cups Sugar
⅔ cup Cold Water
Pinch of Cream of Tartar
2 Egg Whites
2 t. Orange Flower Water
1 cup Chopped, Blanched Almonds

METHOD

❧ Put the honey, sugar, and water in a saucepan over a low heat and stir until it has completely dissolved. Add the cream of tartar, then continue boiling until it reaches 240°F; use a sugar thermometer to take this reading accurately.

❧ Beat the egg whites until they form stiff peaks, then gradually add the sugar solution a little at a time, stirring continuously, until it has all been incorporated. As the sugar cools, it will become harder to beat.

❧ When it has become quite stiff, stir in the orange flower water and the chopped almonds. Pour into buttered pans and mark into squares when cool.

PARSLEY HONEY, A RUSTIC RECIPE FOR SWEET ECONOMY

PARSLEY HONEY
<svg>ᘒᘒᘒ</svg>

*This is a useful way to use parsley that has gone to seed. You could add
the juice of a small lemon in with the sugar. The recipe is a traditional
country one, and produces a syrup rather like thin honey.*

A Royal Cold Cure

THIS WAS what Queen
Victoria and her ladies
drank when afflicted by a
cold. Mix a tablespoon of
barley in a wine glass of
cold water, pour into a
saucepan with $1^1/4$ cups of
white wine, sweeten with
honey, and add a few
cloves. Stir over the heat
for six minutes. Drink hot
before retiring to bed.

INGREDIENTS

Lots Of Fresh Parsley
Cold Water
Sugar

METHOD

❦ Thoroughly wash lots of parsley and pack it into a medium-sized
saucepan. Cover with cold water and place over a high heat to boil for
30 minutes.

❦ Strain off the juices through a jelly bag and for every $2^1/2$ cups of
juice collected, measure out $2^1/4$ cups sugar.

❦ Boil the juice and sugar together over a fierce heat until the mixture
becomes thick, then remove the pan from the heat, and allow to cool
completely before storing in sterilized jars, as you would any other honey.

INDEX